The Art of Kumihimo

A Comprehensive Guide to Traditional Japanese Braiding

PRUDENCE MICHAEL

copyright@2024

TABLE CONTENT

CHAPTER ONE

    INTRODUCTION

    History of Kumihimo

    Types Of Kumihimo

    Materials For Kumihimo

    Tools For Kumihimo

CHAPTER TWO

    Step By Step Guide To Basic Techniques

    Round Braids

    Flat Braids

    Kongo-Gumi (Chain Braids)

    Simple Beaded Braids

CHAPTER THREE

    Step By Step Guide To Intermediate Techniques

    Adding Beads to a Basic Braid

    Creating a Kumihimo Spiral Braid

    Creating a Kumihimo Braided Bracelet with Clasp

CHAPTER FOUR

    Step By Step Guide To Advance Techniques

    Kumihimo Dragon Tail Braid

    Kumihimo Beaded Rope Necklace

    Kumihimo Beaded Spiral Rope

    Designing a Kumihimo Flower Pattern

CHAPTER FIVE
- Step By Step Guide To Beginners Projects
- Kumihimo Keychain
- Simple Kumihimo Bracelet
- Kumihimo Bookmark
- Simple Kumihimo Headband

CHAPTER SIX
- Step By Step Guide To Intermediate Projects
- Kumihimo Lanyard
- Braided Kumihimo Necklace with Beads
- Kumihimo Braided Belt
- Kumihimo Beaded Bracelet with Adjustable Knot

CHAPTER SEVEN
- Step By Step Guide To Advance Projects
- Kumihimo Beaded Dragonfly Brooch
- Kumihimo Multi-Strand Necklace
- Kumihimo Beaded Fringe Necklace
- Kumihimo Beaded Bracelet with Complex Patterns

CHAPTER EIGHT
- Troubleshooting
- General Tips
- Conclusion

CHAPTER ONE

INTRODUCTION

Kumihimo is a traditional Japanese braiding technique used to create intricate and decorative cords or braids. The word "kumihimo" translates to "gathered threads" or "braided cords" in Japanese. The technique has been practiced for centuries and was historically used to create cords for clothing, armor, and other functional items.

Kumihimo typically involves braiding threads or fibers using a round or square disk, a marudai (a traditional braiding stand), or a takadai (a more advanced braiding loom). The braids can vary in complexity, from simple round or flat braids to intricate designs incorporating beads, metallic threads, or multiple colors.

The practice is popular among crafters and textile artists today for making jewelry, decorative items, and accessories.

History of Kumihimo

Kumihimo has a rich history that dates back over a thousand years in Japan. Here's a brief overview:

Origins and Development

Early Use: Kumihimo is believed to have originated in Japan during the Nara period (710-794 AD). Early uses included creating cords for securing armor and clothing, as well as decorative items for ceremonial purposes.

Heian Period (794-1185): The art of kumihimo evolved during the Heian period, with more complex and decorative braids becoming popular in courtly fashion. These braids were often used to adorn clothing and accessories.

Historical Significance

Samurai Armor: Kumihimo played a crucial role in the creation of samurai armor, where the braids were used to secure the armor pieces together and provide flexibility and strength.

Cultural Symbolism: The art of kumihimo is intertwined with Japanese culture and aesthetics, reflecting values such as patience, precision, and beauty.

Tools and Techniques

Marudai and Takadai: Traditional tools like the marudai (a round braiding stand) and the takadai (a more advanced loom) were developed to facilitate the complex braiding patterns used in kumihimo.

Evolution: Over time, kumihimo techniques expanded beyond functional applications to include decorative and artistic braids, leading to a diverse range of styles and patterns.

Modern Era

Revival and Popularity: In recent decades, kumihimo has experienced a revival as a popular craft, with contemporary artists and crafters incorporating the technique into jewelry, accessories, and other creative projects.

Global Reach: Kumihimo has gained international recognition, with workshops, books, and online resources making it accessible to crafters around the world.

Kumihimo's blend of historical significance and artistic expression continues to captivate and inspire people today, maintaining its place as a cherished and versatile craft.

Types Of Kumihimo

Kumihimo includes a variety of braiding techniques and patterns, each producing different types of cords or braids. Here are some common types:

1. Hira-Gumi (Flat Braids)

Description: Flat, often wide braids with a consistent pattern across their surface.

Uses: Often used in decorative belts, straps, and jewelry.

2. Maru-Gumi (Round Braids)

Description: Round in cross-section, these braids can vary in thickness and complexity.

Uses: Commonly used in traditional clothing accessories and modern jewelry.

3. Kongo-Gumi (Chain Braids)

Description: A type of round braid that creates a chain-like appearance with interlocking segments.

Uses: Ideal for creating intricate designs and patterns in jewelry.

4. Tsumami-Kogei (Gathered Braids)

Description: Features gathered or gathered-in patterns, often with decorative elements like beads.

Uses: Used in decorative accessories, often seen in hair ornaments and jewelry.

5. Tatewaku-Gumi (Square Braids)

Description: Braids with a square cross-section, resulting in a more structured and angular appearance.

Uses: Used in accessories and functional items where a square profile is desired.

6. Himo-Kumi (Cord Braids)

Description: Traditional cord braids used for functional and decorative purposes.

Uses: Common in traditional garments and ceremonial items.

7. Ito-Kumi (Thread Braids)

Description: Made using fine threads, these braids can be highly detailed and delicate.

Uses: Often used in intricate jewelry designs and delicate accessories.

8. Hishi-Gumi (Diamond-Shaped Braids)

Description: Creates a diamond or lozenge-shaped pattern in the braid.

Uses: Popular in decorative cords and unique design projects.

Each type of kumihimo braid can be adapted and modified with different materials, colors, and techniques to create a wide range of patterns and applications.

Materials For Kumihimo

Kumihimo braiding involves a variety of materials, each affecting the final appearance and functionality of the braid. Here are some common materials used:

1. Threads and Yarns

Silk: Luxurious and smooth, often used in high-end jewelry and decorative pieces.

Cotton: Durable and versatile, suitable for a range of projects from accessories to functional cords.

Nylon: Strong and flexible, often used in practical applications and for adding strength to the braid.

Wool: Soft and textured, used for cozy and decorative braids.

2. Beads and Embellishments

Glass Beads: Add sparkle and texture; available in various shapes and sizes.

Metallic Beads: Include silver, gold, or brass beads for a touch of elegance.

Gemstones: Precious or semi-precious stones for a luxurious look.

Charms: Decorative elements that can be incorporated into the braid for personalization.

3. Cords and Ribbons

Satin Cords: Smooth and shiny, ideal for a polished look.

Leather Strips: Adds texture and durability; used in both fashion and functional pieces.

Organza Ribbons: Light and airy, often used for decorative purposes.

4. Specialty Threads

Metallic Threads: Include gold or silver threads for added sparkle and sophistication.

Elastic Threads: Provides stretch and flexibility, often used in jewelry and accessories.

5. Braiding Disks and Stands

Kumihimo Disks: Round or square tools with slots for arranging threads, used to create different braiding patterns.

Marudai: A traditional round stand used for more complex braiding techniques.

Takadai: An advanced loom for intricate and elaborate braids.

6. Tools

Bobbins: Small spools used to hold and manage thread or yarn during braiding.

Scissors: For cutting threads and trimming finished braids.

Needles: Often used to weave in ends or add beads to the braid.

Selecting the right materials depends on the desired outcome, whether it's a durable functional braid or a decorative piece with intricate details.

Tools For Kumihimo

To practice kumihimo effectively, you'll need a few essential tools. The following are rundown of the primary tools used:

1. Kumihimo Disk

Description: A round, flat disk with notches or slots around the edges for arranging threads.

Uses: Ideal for creating simple to moderately complex braids. The disk helps manage the threads and maintain consistent tension.

2. Marudai

Description: A traditional round stand with a central pole and cords that hang from it.

Uses: Used for more advanced kumihimo techniques and intricate braids. The marudai allows for more control and precision.

3. Takadai

Description: An advanced, elevated loom with multiple pegs for thread placement.

Uses: Suitable for creating highly complex and detailed braids. The takadai provides a sophisticated setup for intricate patterns.

4. Bobbins

Description: Small spools or reels used to hold and manage threads.

Uses: Keeps threads organized and prevents tangling. Essential for maintaining smooth and consistent braiding.

5. Weights

Description: Small weights used to keep the threads taut during braiding.

Uses: Ensures that the threads remain under tension, which is crucial for maintaining uniform braids. They are often used with the marudai.

6. Scissors

Description: Sharp cutting tools.

Uses: For trimming threads and cutting off excess after braiding.

7. Needles

Description: Small, pointed tools.

Uses: Used to weave in the ends of the braid or to add beads and other embellishments.

8. Thread Conditioner

Description: Products used to treat threads for smoother handling.

Uses: Helps reduce tangling and fraying, making the braiding process smoother.

9. Threading Tools

Description: Tools like threaders or tweezers.

Uses: Assist in threading beads or managing fine threads.

10. Pattern Templates

Description: Printed or digital patterns for braiding.

Uses: Guides for creating specific braiding designs and patterns.

These tools can be used individually or in combination, depending on the complexity of the braid and the desired outcome.

CHAPTER TWO
Basic Techniques

Round Braids

Materials Needed: Origbo emuobo joy, 0020758973 GTB

Kumihimo disk

8 strands of thread or yarn

Scissors

Steps:

Prepare the Threads: Cut 8 strands of thread or yarn, each about 18-24 inches long. Fold them in half and secure the folded ends together with a knot or a small piece of tape.

Set Up the Disk: Place the kumihimo disk on a flat surface. Insert the folded ends of the threads through the center hole of the disk and spread them evenly around the notches, pairing each thread with another in the notches.

Arrange the Threads: Place the threads in the notches in pairs. For example, you can arrange them in the following sequence: 1-3, 2-4, 5-7, 6-8. This means Thread 1 and Thread 3 are in one pair, and so on.

Start Braiding:

Move the Leftmost Thread: Lift the leftmost thread from its notch and move it to the right notch directly opposite.

Move the Rightmost Thread: Lift the rightmost thread and move it to the left notch directly opposite.

Rotate the Disk: Rotate the disk 90 degrees to the right to reposition the threads.

Repeat: Continue moving the leftmost and rightmost threads, rotating the disk each time, until the braid reaches the desired length.

Finish the Braid: Once you've reached the desired length, carefully remove the braid from the disk. Tie a knot at the end to secure the threads, then trim any excess.

Flat Braids

Materials Needed:

Kumihimo disk (or a square board for a flat braid)

8 strands of thread or yarn

Scissors

Steps:

Prepare the Threads: Cut 8 strands of thread or yarn, each about 18-24 inches long. Fold them in half and secure the folded ends together with a knot or tape.

Set Up the Disk: Place the kumihimo disk or square board on a flat surface. Insert the folded ends of the threads through the center hole and arrange them around the notches or pegs. For a flat braid, you may need to use a square board or adjust the disk setup.

Arrange the Threads: For a basic flat braid, arrange the threads in a repeating pattern. For example, you can place threads 1 and 3 in one row, threads 2 and 4 in another, and so on.

Start Braiding:

Move the Top Row: Lift the top row of threads and move them to the bottom row directly below.

Move the Bottom Row: Lift the bottom row of threads and move them to the top row directly above.

Repeat: Continue alternating between the top and bottom rows, ensuring each thread moves to its new position, until the braid is the desired length.

Finish the Braid: Once the braid reaches the desired length, carefully remove it from the disk or board. Tie a knot at the end to secure the threads, then trim any excess.

Kongo-Gumi (Chain Braids)

Materials Needed:

Kumihimo disk

8 strands of thread or yarn (or more for a more complex braid)

Scissors

Steps:

Prepare the Threads: Cut 8 strands of thread, each about 18-24 inches long. Fold them in half and secure the folded ends with a knot or tape.

Set Up the Disk: Place the kumihimo disk on a flat surface. Insert the folded ends through the center hole and arrange them around the notches. For a Kongo-Gumi braid, place threads in a pattern like 1-4, 2-5, 3-6, 4-7.

Arrange the Threads: Position the threads around the disk. For a basic Kongo-Gumi, arrange them so that the strands alternate between top and bottom positions around the disk.

Start Braiding:

Move the Leftmost Thread: Lift the leftmost thread from its notch and move it to the opposite notch directly across the disk.

Move the Rightmost Thread: Lift the rightmost thread and move it to the opposite notch directly across.

Rotate the Disk: Rotate the disk 90 degrees to the right after each set of moves.

Repeat: Continue moving the leftmost and rightmost threads, rotating the disk, until the braid reaches the desired length.

Finish the Braid: Once the braid is the desired length, remove it from the disk, tie a knot to secure the ends, and trim any excess threads.

Simple Beaded Braids

Materials Needed:

Kumihimo disk

8 strands of thread or yarn

Beads (with large enough holes to fit the thread)

Scissors

Steps:

Prepare the Threads: Cut 8 strands of thread, each about 18-24 inches long. Thread beads onto each strand before starting, if using beads throughout the braid.

Set Up the Disk: Place the kumihimo disk on a flat surface. Insert the strands through the center hole and arrange them around the notches.

Arrange the Threads: Position the threads around the disk. Make sure to distribute the beads evenly or as desired.

Start Braiding:

Move the Leftmost Thread: Lift the leftmost thread from its notch and move it to the opposite notch directly across the disk.

Move the Rightmost Thread: Lift the rightmost thread and move it to the opposite notch directly across.

Insert Beads (Optional): If adding beads periodically, slide a bead onto the thread as you move it. Ensure the beads do not get caught or tangled.

Rotate the Disk: Rotate the disk 90 degrees to the right after each set of moves.

Repeat: Continue braiding and adding beads until the braid reaches the desired length.

Finish the Braid: Remove the braid from the disk, tie a knot to secure the ends, and trim any excess threads.

These guides should help you get started with basic kumihimo techniques. Feel free to experiment with different colors and materials to create unique designs!

CHAPTER THREE
Intermediate Techniques

Adding Beads to a Basic Braid

Materials Needed:

Kumihimo disk

8 strands of thread or yarn

Beads (with large enough holes to fit the thread)

Scissors

Steps:

Prepare the Threads: Cut 8 strands of thread, each about 18-24 inches long. Thread beads onto each strand before starting, or plan to add beads during the braiding process.

Set Up the Disk: Place the kumihimo disk on a flat surface. Insert the ends of the threads through the center hole and arrange them around the notches. Ensure that the beads are evenly distributed or placed as desired.

Arrange the Threads: For a basic braid, arrange the threads around the disk in pairs. For example, if you're using a round disk, you might arrange them in pairs like this: 1-3, 2-4, 5-7, 6-8.

Start Braiding:

Move the Leftmost Thread: Lift the leftmost thread from its notch and move it to the opposite notch directly across the disk.

Move the Rightmost Thread: Lift the rightmost thread and move it to the opposite notch directly across.

Insert Beads (During Braiding): When you reach a bead, slide it up the thread before moving it to the opposite notch. Make sure the bead is positioned as desired in the braid.

Rotate the Disk: Rotate the disk 90 degrees to the right after each set of moves.

Repeat: Continue braiding, ensuring beads are incorporated into the braid as you go.

Finish the Braid: Once you've reached the desired length, remove the braid from the disk, tie a knot to secure the ends, and trim any excess threads.

Creating a Kumihimo Spiral Braid

Materials Needed:

Kumihimo disk

8 strands of thread or yarn (preferably in different colors for a more pronounced spiral effect)

Scissors

Steps:

Prepare the Threads: Cut 8 strands of thread, each about 18-24 inches long. Arrange them so that you have a mix of colors or patterns for a more visible spiral.

Set Up the Disk: Place the kumihimo disk on a flat surface. Insert the threads through the center hole and arrange them around the notches in the following pattern: 1-3, 2-4, 5-7, 6-8. Each pair should be alternating in color or pattern.

Arrange the Threads: Position the threads in the notches so that they alternate between different colors or patterns.

Start Braiding:

Move the Leftmost Thread: Lift the leftmost thread from its notch and move it to the notch directly across the disk.

Move the Rightmost Thread: Lift the rightmost thread and move it to the notch directly across.

Rotate the Disk: Rotate the disk 90 degrees to the right after each set of moves.

Repeat: Continue moving the threads and rotating the disk. The alternating colors and patterns will naturally create a spiral effect as you braid.

Finish the Braid: Once the braid reaches the desired length, remove it from the disk, tie a knot to secure the ends, and trim any excess threads.

Creating a Kumihimo Braided Bracelet with Clasp

Materials Needed:

Kumihimo disk

8 strands of thread or yarn (for a thicker braid) or 4 strands (for a thinner braid)

Beads (optional)

Jewelry clasp (lobster clasp or toggle clasp)

Jump rings

Scissors

Needle and thread or glue (for securing the clasp)

Steps:

Prepare the Threads: Cut 8 strands of thread, each about 18-24 inches long (or 4 strands if you prefer a thinner braid). If using beads, thread them onto the strands before starting.

Set Up the Disk: Place the kumihimo disk on a flat surface. Insert the threads through the center hole and arrange them around the notches. For an 8-strand braid, arrange them as follows: 1-3, 2-4, 5-7, 6-8.

Arrange the Threads: Position the threads in the notches. If using beads, position them so they are evenly distributed or place them at intervals along the braid.

Start Braiding:

Move the Leftmost Thread: Lift the leftmost thread from its notch and move it to the opposite notch directly across the disk.

Move the Rightmost Thread: Lift the rightmost thread and move it to the opposite notch directly across.

Rotate the Disk: Rotate the disk 90 degrees to the right after each set of moves.

Repeat: Continue braiding until the braid is slightly longer than the circumference of your wrist.

Finish the Braid: Carefully remove the braid from the disk. Tie a knot at each end to prevent unraveling.

Attach the Clasp:

Secure the Ends: Use a needle and thread or glue to secure the ends of the braid to the jewelry clasp. If using glue, ensure it dries completely before handling.

Add Jump Rings: Attach jump rings to the ends of the clasp if necessary, then connect the clasp to the braid.

Trim Excess: Trim any excess thread and ensure the clasp is securely attached.

Check Fit: Try on the bracelet and make any adjustments if needed.

This technique will help you create a stylish kumihimo bracelet with a professional-looking clasp, adding a functional and fashionable touch to your kumihimo projects.

CHAPTER FOUR
Advance Techniques

Kumihimo Dragon Tail Braid

Materials Needed:

Kumihimo disk

8 strands of thread or yarn (using two different colors is helpful)

Scissors

Steps:

Prepare the Threads: Cut 8 strands of thread, each about 18-24 inches long. Use two different colors to create a more pronounced pattern (e.g., 4 strands of each color).

Set Up the Disk: Place the kumihimo disk on a flat surface. Insert the ends of the threads through the center hole, arranging them around the notches. For a Dragon Tail Braid, arrange the threads in an alternating color pattern. Place them like this: 1-5, 2-6, 3-7, 4-8.

Arrange the Threads: Ensure that the threads are evenly distributed and that the color pattern is clear.

Start Braiding:

Move the Leftmost Thread: Lift the leftmost thread and move it to the opposite notch directly across the disk. If the thread is a different color, this will create a pattern as you move threads.

Move the Rightmost Thread: Lift the rightmost thread and move it to the opposite notch directly across.

Rotate the Disk: Rotate the disk 90 degrees to the right after each set of moves.

Repeat: Continue this process. The Dragon Tail Braid pattern will emerge as the threads intertwine, creating a distinctive, intricate design.

Finish the Braid: Once the braid reaches the desired length, carefully remove it from the disk. Tie knots at both ends to secure the braid and trim any excess thread.

Kumihimo Beaded Rope Necklace

Materials Needed:

Kumihimo disk

8 strands of thread or yarn

Beads with large enough holes

Jewelry clasp (lobster clasp or toggle clasp)

Jump rings

Scissors

Needle and thread or glue (for securing the clasp)

Steps:

Prepare the Threads and Beads: Cut 8 strands of thread, each about 18-24 inches long. Thread beads onto each strand, leaving space for braiding. Ensure the beads fit easily on the threads.

Set Up the Disk: Place the kumihimo disk on a flat surface. Insert the threads through the center hole, arranging them around the notches. You can mix colors or keep them uniform, depending on your design preference.

Arrange the Threads: Position the threads around the disk, placing beads in an evenly distributed pattern. Be mindful of how beads will affect the braiding pattern.

Start Braiding:

Move the Leftmost Thread: Lift the leftmost thread with a bead and move it to the opposite notch. The bead should slide into the braid.

Move the Rightmost Thread: Lift the rightmost thread with a bead and move it to the opposite notch.

Rotate the Disk: Rotate the disk 90 degrees to the right after each set of moves.

Repeat: Continue braiding, ensuring that beads are incorporated into the braid as you progress. Adjust bead placement as needed to create a balanced pattern.

Finish the Necklace: Once the braid reaches the desired length, carefully remove it from the disk. Tie knots at both ends to secure the braid and trim any excess thread.

Attach the Clasp:

Secure the Ends: Use a needle and thread or glue to attach the ends of the braid to the jewelry clasp. Allow glue to dry completely if used.

Add Jump Rings: Attach jump rings to the clasp and connect them to the braid if necessary.

Kumihimo Beaded Spiral Rope

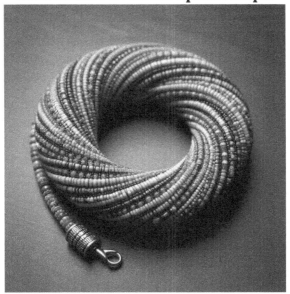

Materials Needed:

Kumihimo disk

8 strands of thread or yarn

Beads (with large enough holes)

Scissors

Steps:

Prepare the Threads and Beads: Cut 8 strands of thread, each about 18-24 inches long. Thread beads onto each strand, making sure they fit over the thread without obstructing the braiding process.

Set Up the Disk: Place the kumihimo disk on a flat surface. Insert the threads through the center hole and arrange them around the notches. Distribute the beads evenly among the threads.

Arrange the Threads: Position the threads around the disk in pairs. For a spiral effect, ensure the beads are evenly spaced or alternated in color.

Start Braiding:

Move the Leftmost Thread: Lift the leftmost thread and move it to the opposite notch. Beads should slide into the braid as you move the thread.

Move the Rightmost Thread: Lift the rightmost thread and move it to the opposite notch.

Rotate the Disk: Rotate the disk 90 degrees to the right after each set of moves.

Repeat: Continue braiding, ensuring that beads are incorporated and positioned to create a spiral pattern.

Finish the Rope: Once the spiral braid reaches the desired length, carefully remove it from the disk. Tie knots at both ends to secure the braid and trim any excess thread.

Designing a Kumihimo Flower Pattern

Materials Needed:

Kumihimo disk

8 strands of thread or yarn in various colors

Scissors

Steps:

Prepare the Threads: Cut 8 strands of thread, each about 18-24 inches long, in multiple colors if you want a colorful pattern. Arrange them so that each color will appear in the final flower design.

Set Up the Disk: Place the kumihimo disk on a flat surface. Insert the threads through the center hole and arrange them around the notches in a pattern that will form the flower shape. For instance, place threads in an alternating color pattern that mimics petal shapes.

Arrange the Threads: Position the threads in a way that will create a flower-like pattern. For example, you can place threads in a sequence such as: 1-4, 2-5, 3-6, 7-8.

Start Braiding:

Move the Leftmost Thread: Lift the leftmost thread from its notch and move it to the opposite notch across the disk.

Move the Rightmost Thread: Lift the rightmost thread and move it to the opposite notch.

Rotate the Disk: Rotate the disk 90 degrees to the right after each set of moves.

Repeat: Continue this process, focusing on maintaining the pattern that will produce the flower shape. Adjust thread movement and rotation as needed to perfect the flower design.

Finish the Pattern: Once the flower pattern is complete and reaches the desired length, carefully remove it from the disk. Tie knots at both ends to secure the braid and trim any excess thread.

These advanced techniques will help you create intricate and beautiful kumihimo designs, adding a unique touch to your crafting projects.

CHAPTER FIVE
Beginners Projects

Kumihimo Keychain

Materials Needed:

Kumihimo disk

8 strands of thread or yarn (each about 18 inches long)

Keychain ring or clip

Scissors

Optional: beads or charms

Steps:

Prepare the Threads: Cut 8 strands of thread or yarn, each approximately 18 inches long. If desired, thread a few beads onto some of the strands for added decoration.

Set Up the Disk: Place the kumihimo disk on a flat surface. Insert the ends of the threads through the center hole and arrange them around the notches in the following pattern: 1-3, 2-4, 5-7, 6-8.

Arrange the Threads: Distribute the threads evenly in the notches. If using beads, ensure they are placed at regular intervals or at the ends of the threads.

Start Braiding:

Move the Leftmost Thread: Lift the leftmost thread and move it to the notch directly opposite.

Move the Rightmost Thread: Lift the rightmost thread and move it to the notch directly opposite.

Rotate the Disk: Rotate the disk 90 degrees to the right after each set of moves.

Repeat: Continue braiding until the keychain reaches the desired length, usually about 4-6 inches.

Finish the Keychain: Once the braid is long enough, remove it from the disk. To keep the threads in place, tie a knot at the end. Attach the braided keychain to the keychain ring or clip.

Optional: Add any additional beads or charms to the braid for extra decoration before tying the final knot.

Simple Kumihimo Bracelet

Materials Needed:

Kumihimo disk

8 strands of thread or yarn (each about 18 inches long)

Jewelry clasp (lobster clasp or toggle clasp)

Jump rings

Scissors

Optional: beads

Steps:

Prepare the Threads: Cut 8 strands of thread or yarn, each approximately 18 inches long. If you want a beaded bracelet, thread beads onto some of the strands.

Set Up the Disk: Place the kumihimo disk on a flat surface. Insert the ends of the threads through the center hole and arrange them around the notches. For a simple braid, use a pattern like: 1-3, 2-4, 5-7, 6-8.

Arrange the Threads: Position the threads evenly in the notches. If using beads, ensure they are spaced out or positioned at regular intervals.

Start Braiding:

Move the Leftmost Thread: Lift the leftmost thread and move it to the opposite notch.

Move the Rightmost Thread: Lift the rightmost thread and move it to the opposite notch.

Rotate the Disk: Rotate the disk 90 degrees to the right after each set of moves.

Repeat: Continue braiding until the bracelet is the desired length, typically around 6-8 inches, depending on wrist size.

Finish the Bracelet: Once the braid reaches the desired length, remove it from the disk. Tie a knot at each end to secure the threads.

Attach the Clasp:

Secure the Ends: Use a needle and thread or glue to attach the ends of the braid to the jewelry clasp. Allow glue to dry completely if used.

Add Jump Rings: Attach jump rings to the clasp and connect them to the braid.

Kumihimo Bookmark

Materials Needed:

Kumihimo disk

8 strands of thread or yarn (each about 18 inches long)

A decorative tassel or charm (optional)

Scissors

Steps:

Prepare the Threads: Cut 8 strands of thread or yarn, each about 18 inches long.

Choose colors that you like and cut the threads evenly.

Set Up the Disk: Place the kumihimo disk on a flat surface. Insert the ends of the threads through the center hole and arrange them around the notches. Use a pattern such as: 1-3, 2-4, 5-7, 6-8.

Arrange the Threads: Position the threads in the notches evenly. Ensure that they are not tangled and are distributed in a balanced way.

Start Braiding:

Move the Leftmost Thread: Lift the leftmost thread and move it to the notch directly opposite.

Move the Rightmost Thread: Lift the rightmost thread and move it to the notch directly opposite.

Rotate the Disk: Rotate the disk 90 degrees to the right after each set of moves.

Repeat: Continue braiding until the bookmark reaches the desired length, generally around 6-8 inches.

Finish the Bookmark: Once you reach the desired length, remove the braid from the disk. Tie a knot at each end to prevent unraveling.

Add a Tassel or Charm (Optional): Attach a decorative tassel or charm to one end of the bookmark for added flair.

Simple Kumihimo Headband

Materials Needed:

Kumihimo disk

8 strands of thread or yarn (each about 24 inches long)

Scissors

Optional: beads or decorative elements

Steps:

Prepare the Threads: Cut 8 strands of thread or yarn, each about 24 inches long. If you want to add beads, thread them onto some of the strands.

Set Up the Disk: Place the kumihimo disk on a flat surface. Insert the ends of the threads through the center hole and arrange them around the notches in a pattern like: 1-3, 2-4, 5-7, 6-8.

Arrange the Threads: Position the threads evenly in the notches. Beads can be added at regular intervals if desired.

Start Braiding:

Move the Leftmost Thread: Lift the leftmost thread and move it to the notch directly opposite.

Move the Rightmost Thread: Lift the rightmost thread and move it to the notch directly opposite.

Rotate the Disk: Rotate the disk 90 degrees to the right after each set of moves.

Repeat: Continue braiding until the headband reaches the desired length, usually around 15-18 inches, depending on head size.

Finish the Headband: Once the braid is long enough, remove it from the disk. Tie a knot at each end to secure the threads.

Adjust the Size: Try the headband on to ensure it fits. You can adjust the length or add additional decorations if needed.

These beginner projects are both practical and fun, giving you a chance to create useful and stylish items while mastering basic kumihimo techniques.

CHAPTER SIX
Intermediate Projects

Kumihimo Lanyard

Materials Needed:

Kumihimo disk

8 strands of thread or yarn (each about 36 inches long for a lanyard)

Lobster clasp or keyring

Scissors

Steps:

Prepare the Threads: Cut 8 strands of thread or yarn, each approximately 36 inches long. Choose colors or patterns that you like.

Set Up the Disk: Place the kumihimo disk on a flat surface. Insert the ends of the threads through the center hole and arrange them around the notches in a pattern such as: 1-3, 2-4, 5-7, 6-8.

Arrange the Threads: Position the threads evenly around the disk. Ensure that they are not tangled and are distributed evenly.

Start Braiding:

Move the Leftmost Thread: Lift the leftmost thread and move it to the opposite notch.

Move the Rightmost Thread: Lift the rightmost thread and move it to the opposite notch.

Rotate the Disk: Rotate the disk 90 degrees to the right after each set of moves.

Repeat: Continue braiding until the lanyard reaches the desired length, usually around 18-24 inches.

Finish the Lanyard: Once the braid reaches the desired length, remove it from the disk. Tie a knot at each end to prevent unraveling.

Attach the Clasp: Use a jump ring or directly attach a lobster clasp or keyring to one end of the lanyard. Secure the clasp with a knot or glue if needed.

Braided Kumihimo Necklace with Beads

Materials Needed:

Kumihimo disk

8 strands of thread or yarn (each about 24 inches long)

Beads with large holes

Necklace clasp (lobster clasp or toggle clasp)

Jump rings

Scissors

Steps:

Prepare the Threads and Beads: Cut 8 strands of thread, each about 24 inches long. Thread beads onto each strand, leaving space for braiding.

Set Up the Disk: Place the kumihimo disk on a flat surface. Insert the threads through the center hole and arrange them around the notches. Distribute the beads evenly or as desired.

Arrange the Threads: Position the threads in the notches, ensuring that beads are distributed evenly or are placed at regular intervals.

Start Braiding:

Move the Leftmost Thread: Lift the leftmost thread and move it to the opposite notch. Beads should slide into the braid as you move the thread.

Move the Rightmost Thread: Lift the rightmost thread and move it to the opposite notch.

Rotate the Disk: Rotate the disk 90 degrees to the right after each set of moves.

Repeat: Continue braiding until the necklace reaches the desired length, usually around 18-20 inches.

Finish the Necklace: Once the braid is long enough, remove it from the disk. To keep the braid in place, tie knots at both ends.

Attach the Clasp:

Secure the Ends: Use a needle and thread or glue to attach the ends of the braid to the necklace clasp. Allow glue to dry completely if used.

Add Jump Rings: Attach jump rings to the clasp and connect them to the braid if necessary.

Kumihimo Braided Belt

Materials Needed:

Kumihimo disk

8 strands of thread or yarn (each about 60 inches long, depending on the desired belt length)

Belt buckle or decorative end pieces

Scissors

Steps:

Prepare the Threads: Cut 8 strands of thread or yarn, each about 60 inches long.

Pick hues and designs that go with your personal style.

Set Up the Disk: Place the kumihimo disk on a flat surface. Insert the ends of the threads through the center hole and arrange them around the notches in a pattern such as: 1-3, 2-4, 5-7, 6-8.

Arrange the Threads: Ensure the threads are evenly distributed in the notches. They should not be tangled and should be properly positioned for braiding.

Start Braiding:

Move the Leftmost Thread: Lift the leftmost thread and move it to the opposite notch.

Move the Rightmost Thread: Lift the rightmost thread and move it to the opposite notch.

Rotate the Disk: Rotate the disk 90 degrees to the right after each set of moves.

Repeat: Continue braiding until the belt reaches the desired length. Depending on the width and complexity of the braid, this might take some time.

Finish the Belt: Once the braid is complete, remove it from the disk. Tie a knot at each end to prevent unraveling.

Attach the Buckle:

Secure the Ends: Attach the braid ends to the belt buckle or decorative end pieces using glue or sewing them in place. Ensure they are securely fastened.

Kumihimo Beaded Bracelet with Adjustable Knot

Materials Needed:

Kumihimo disk

8 strands of thread or yarn (each about 24 inches long)

Beads with large enough holes

Scissors

Sliding knot or adjustable cord lock

Steps:

Prepare the Threads and Beads: Cut 8 strands of thread, each about 24 inches long. Thread beads onto each strand, leaving some space for braiding.

Set Up the Disk: Place the kumihimo disk on a flat surface. Insert the threads through the center hole and arrange them around the notches. Distribute the beads evenly or as desired.

Arrange the Threads: Position the threads in the notches, ensuring that the beads are evenly distributed or placed according to your design.

Start Braiding:

Move the Leftmost Thread: Lift the leftmost thread and move it to the opposite notch. Beads should slide into the braid as you move the thread.

Move the Rightmost Thread: Lift the rightmost thread and move it to the opposite notch.

Rotate the Disk: Rotate the disk 90 degrees to the right after each set of moves.

Repeat: Continue braiding until the bracelet is the desired length.

Finish the Bracelet: Once the braid reaches the desired length, remove it from the disk. Tie knots at each end to secure the threads.

Add the Adjustable Knot:

Attach the Sliding Knot or Cord Lock: To make the bracelet adjustable, attach a sliding knot or cord lock to each end. If using a sliding knot, tie it at each end of the bracelet to allow for size adjustments. If using a cord lock, thread the end of the braid through the lock and secure it.

These projects provide additional practice with kumihimo techniques while allowing you to create functional and stylish items.

CHAPTER SEVEN
Advance Projects

Kumihimo Beaded Dragonfly Brooch

Materials Needed:

Kumihimo disk

8 strands of thread or yarn (each about 24 inches long)

Small beads for the body and wings

Brooch pin back

Needle and thread

Scissors

Optional: metallic thread or wire for additional accents

Steps:

Prepare the Threads and Beads: Cut 8 strands of thread, each about 24 inches long. Select beads for the dragonfly's body and wings, making sure they fit on the thread.

Set Up the Disk: Place the kumihimo disk on a flat surface. Insert the threads through the center hole and arrange them around the notches. Distribute the beads according to your design, such as alternating colors for the body and wings.

Arrange the Threads: Position the threads evenly in the notches, placing beads where they will be incorporated into the braid.

Start Braiding:

Move the Leftmost Thread: Lift the leftmost thread and move it to the opposite notch. Beads should slide into the braid as you move the thread.

Move the Rightmost Thread: Lift the rightmost thread and move it to the opposite notch.

Rotate the Disk: Rotate the disk 90 degrees to the right after each set of moves.

Repeat: Continue braiding until the desired length for the dragonfly's body is achieved.

Shape the Dragonfly: Remove the braid from the disk. Shape the braided section into the dragonfly's body and wings. Use additional thread or wire to add details or enhance the shape if needed.

Attach the Brooch Pin:

Secure the Brooch Pin: Use a needle and thread to sew or glue the brooch pin back to the back of the dragonfly. Ensure it is securely attached.

Finish: Trim any excess thread and make final adjustments to the shape of the dragonfly.

Kumihimo Multi-Strand Necklace

Materials Needed:

Kumihimo disk

24 strands of thread or yarn (6 strands per color for a 4-strand braid, with 4 colors)

Beads or decorative elements

Necklace clasp (lobster clasp or toggle clasp)

Jump rings

Scissors

Steps:

Prepare the Threads and Beads: Cut 24 strands of thread, each about 24 inches long. Divide them into 4 groups of 6 strands each. Thread beads onto some of the strands if desired.

Set Up the Disk: Place the kumihimo disk on a flat surface. Insert the ends of the threads through the center hole and arrange them in groups around the notches. Use a pattern that will create a multi-strand effect when braided.

Arrange the Threads: Distribute the threads evenly in the notches, ensuring that beads or decorative elements are positioned as desired.

Start Braiding:

Move the Leftmost Thread: Lift the leftmost thread from each group and move it to the opposite notch.

Move the Rightmost Thread: Lift the rightmost thread from each group and move it to the opposite notch.

Rotate the Disk: Rotate the disk 90 degrees to the right after each set of moves.

Repeat: Continue braiding until the necklace reaches the desired length, usually around 18-20 inches.

Finish the Necklace: Once the braid is complete, remove it from the disk. Tie knots at each end to prevent unraveling.

Attach the Clasp:

Secure the Ends: Use a needle and thread or glue to attach the ends of the braid to the necklace clasp. Allow glue to dry completely if used.

Add Jump Rings: Attach jump rings to the clasp and connect them to the braid if necessary.

Kumihimo Beaded Fringe Necklace

Materials Needed:

Kumihimo disk

8 strands of thread or yarn (each about 24 inches long)

Beads in various sizes and shapes (for fringe and body)

Necklace clasp (lobster clasp or toggle clasp)

Jump rings

Scissors

Steps:

Prepare the Threads and Beads: Cut 8 strands of thread, each about 24 inches long. Choose beads for the main braid and additional fringe. Thread beads onto the strands if desired.

Set Up the Disk: Place the kumihimo disk on a flat surface. Insert the ends of the threads through the center hole and arrange them around the notches in a pattern such as: 1-3, 2-4, 5-7, 6-8.

Arrange the Threads: Distribute the beads evenly or as desired. Position them so that they will be incorporated into the braid.

Start Braiding:

Move the Leftmost Thread: Lift the leftmost thread and move it to the opposite notch. Beads should slide into the braid as you move the thread.

Move the Rightmost Thread: Lift the rightmost thread and move it to the opposite notch.

Rotate the Disk: Rotate the disk 90 degrees to the right after each set of moves.

Repeat: Continue braiding until the necklace reaches the desired length.

Create the Fringe:

Add Fringe: Once the main braid is complete, attach additional beads or strands to the ends of the necklace to create fringe. You can knot or glue the beads in place.

Attach the Clasp:

Secure the Ends: Use a needle and thread or glue to attach the ends of the braid to the necklace clasp. If you're using glue, let it totally dry.

Add Jump Rings: Attach jump rings to the clasp and connect them to the braid if necessary.

Kumihimo Beaded Bracelet with Complex Patterns

Materials Needed:

Kumihimo disk

8 strands of thread or yarn (each about 24 inches long)

Beads with varying sizes and patterns

Bracelet clasp (lobster clasp or toggle clasp)

Jump rings

Scissors

Steps:

Prepare the Threads and Beads: Cut 8 strands of thread, each about 24 inches long. Select beads in different sizes and patterns. Thread beads onto some of the strands for intricate patterns.

Set Up the Disk: Place the kumihimo disk on a flat surface. Insert the threads through the center hole and arrange them around the notches in a complex pattern that complements your bead arrangement. For For instance, use gradient effects or color alternating.

Arrange the Threads: Position the threads evenly in the notches, ensuring the beads are distributed as desired for your pattern.

Start Braiding:

Move the Leftmost Thread: Lift the leftmost thread and move it to the opposite notch. The beads should follow the braiding pattern and create a complex design.

Move the Rightmost Thread: Lift the rightmost thread and move it to the opposite notch.

Rotate the Disk: Rotate the disk 90 degrees to the right after each set of moves.

Repeat: Continue braiding until the bracelet reaches the desired length.

Finish the Bracelet:

Secure the Ends: Remove the braid from the disk and tie knots at each end to prevent unraveling.

Attach the Clasp:

Secure the Ends: Use a needle and thread or glue to attach the ends of the braid to the bracelet clasp. If you're using glue, let it totally dry.

Add Jump Rings: Attach jump rings to the clasp and connect them to the braid if necessary.

These advanced projects incorporate more complex techniques and patterns, showcasing your kumihimo skills while creating beautiful, intricate accessories.

CHAPTER EIGHT

Troubleshooting

Some common kumihimo troubleshooting tips for issues you might encounter during your projects:

1. Tangled Threads

Problem: Threads get tangled or knotted during braiding.

Solutions:

Check Tension: Ensure that the threads are not too tight or too loose. Maintaining consistent tension helps prevent tangling.

Use a Thread Separator: Use thread separators or clips to keep the strands organized and prevent them from tangling.

Untangle Carefully: If tangling occurs, gently untangle the threads by working from the ends and avoiding pulling too hard.

2. Uneven Braid

Problem: The braid appears uneven or lopsided.

Solutions:

Ensure Even Thread Placement: Make sure the threads are evenly distributed in the notches of the kumihimo disk.

Rotate Consistently: Always rotate the disk 90 degrees to the right after each set of moves. Inconsistent rotation can cause uneven braiding.

Check for Loose Threads: Ensure no threads are slipping out of their notches and adjust as necessary.

3. Beads Not Sliding Properly

Problem: Beads get stuck or do not slide smoothly on the threads.

Solutions:

Check Bead Size: Ensure that the beads have large enough holes for the threads to pass through easily.

Use a Bead Threading Tool: If beads are difficult to thread, use a bead threading tool or a needle to help thread them onto the yarn.

Adjust Bead Placement: Make sure beads are positioned correctly and are not causing blockages in the braid.

4. Loose Ends or Unraveling

Problem: The ends of the braid start to unravel or look loose.

Solutions:

Tie Secure Knots: After finishing your braid, tie secure knots at the ends to prevent unraveling.

Use Fray Check: Apply a small amount of fabric glue or fray check to the ends of the threads to secure them.

Finish with End Caps: Use end caps or crimps to neatly finish the ends of the braid and attach clasps or other findings.

5. Braid Not Laying Flat

Problem: The braid is twisting or curling, not laying flat.

Solutions:

Adjust Tension: Ensure that the tension is even throughout the braid. Too tight or too loose tension can cause twisting.

Use a Thread Conditioner: Apply a thread conditioner or beeswax to the threads to reduce friction and help the braid lay flat.

Press or Iron: Gently press or iron the finished braid under a cloth to flatten it, being careful not to damage the threads.

6. Braid Length Issues

Problem: The braid is not the desired length or is too short.

Solutions:

Measure Before Starting: Measure the length of the braid frequently during braiding to ensure it is reaching the desired length.

Add Extra Threads: If you run out of thread, you can add extra threads and continue braiding, securing the ends properly to avoid unraveling.

7. Incorrect Patterns

Problem: The braided pattern does not match the intended design.

Solutions:

Check Pattern Placement: Ensure that the threads are placed in the correct notches according to the pattern you are following.

Verify Moves: Double-check each step of the braiding process to ensure you are moving the correct threads in the correct sequence.

By addressing these common issues, you can achieve smoother results and maintain the quality of your kumihimo projects.

General Tips

Some general tips to help you get the most out of your kumihimo projects:

1. Choose the Right Threads

Quality Matters: Use high-quality threads or yarns that are durable and suitable for kumihimo braiding. Cotton, silk, and satin cords are popular choices.

Match the Thickness: Ensure the thread thickness is appropriate for the size of your kumihimo disk and the type of project you're working on.

2. Maintain Consistent Tension

Avoid Over-Tightening: Keep the tension even, but not too tight, to ensure a smooth and consistent braid.

Check Regularly: Periodically check the tension throughout the braiding process to avoid any inconsistencies.

3. Prepare Your Workspace

Flat Surface: Work on a flat, stable surface to keep the kumihimo disk steady and prevent the threads from tangling.

Good Lighting: Ensure you have good lighting to easily see the details of your work and avoid mistakes.

4. Use the Right Tools

Kumihimo Disk or Marudai: Use a proper kumihimo disk or marudai depending on the complexity of your project.

Scissors and Tools: Keep sharp scissors, beading needles, and other tools handy for trimming and adding details.

5. Practice and Patience

Start Simple: Begin with basic projects to get comfortable with the braiding technique before moving on to more complex designs.

Be Patient: Kumihimo requires patience and practice. Take your time to master the technique and enjoy the process.

6. Keep Threads Organized

Avoid Tangling: Use thread organizers or clips to keep multiple strands separated and prevent tangling.

Manage Long Threads: If working with long threads, keep them organized by using bobbins or wrapping them on a spool.

7. Experiment with Patterns

Try Different Designs: Experiment with various patterns and techniques to expand your skills and create unique designs.

Use Reference Guides: Refer to pattern guides or books to explore new braiding methods and styles.

8. Secure Your Work

Finish Properly: Secure the ends of your braid with knots, glue, or end caps to prevent unraveling.

Attach Findings: Use appropriate findings and clasps for a professional finish on jewelry projects.

9. Clean and Maintain Tools

Keep Clean: Regularly clean your kumihimo disk, tools, and work area to avoid any debris that could affect your braiding.

Store Properly: Store your kumihimo supplies in a clean, dry place to maintain their condition and longevity.

10. Learn from Mistakes

Correct Errors: If you make a mistake, don't get discouraged. Take what you can from it and change it accordingly.

Seek Feedback: Share your work with others or join a kumihimo group to get feedback and improve your skills.

By following these tips, you can enhance your kumihimo experience, improve your technique, and create beautiful, intricate designs with confidence.

CONCLUSION

Kumihimo is a captivating and versatile form of Japanese braiding that offers endless creative possibilities. Whether you're a beginner or an advanced practitioner, mastering kumihimo can be both a rewarding and enjoyable experience.

To summarize:

Understand the Basics: Familiarize yourself with the history, materials, and tools of kumihimo. This foundational knowledge will enhance your crafting experience and help you make informed choices.

Start with Simple Projects: Begin with basic projects to practice your technique. Simple designs like bracelets and bookmarks allow you to build confidence and skill.

Progress to Intermediate Techniques: As you gain proficiency, challenge yourself with more complex projects such as lanyards and beaded necklaces. These projects will introduce you to new techniques and patterns.

Explore Advanced Creations: For those seeking a challenge, advanced projects like intricate brooches and multi-strand necklaces offer opportunities to showcase your expertise and creativity.

Troubleshoot and Refine: Address common issues and continuously refine your skills. Troubleshooting tips and general best practices can help you overcome obstacles and improve your results.

Embrace Creativity: Experiment with different patterns, materials, and designs. Kumihimo allows for a wide range of artistic expression, so don't hesitate to explore and innovate.

With patience and practice, you can master kumihimo and create stunning, personalized pieces that reflect your unique style. Enjoy the journey of learning and crafting with this beautiful art form.

www.ingramcontent.com/pod-product-compliance
Lightning Source LLC
LaVergne TN
LVHW021305080225
803268LV00010BA/1034